Drag Racing
Attacking the Green

By Susan Sexton

Perfection Learning®

Designers: Emily J. Greazel and Nancy Suits

Dedication

For Tyler, best of luck in your racing career!
-SS

Image Credits:
National Hot Rod Association (NHRA) pp. 4, 5, 6–7, 8, 10, 11, 18, 24, 26, 27, 28, 32, 32–33, 33, 36 (bottom), 36–37, 38, 38–39, 39, 40–41, 42, 46, 50, 51, 52, 53, 54, 56, 57, 60

ArtToday pp. 3, 25, 30, 31, 44–45;
Corel Professional Photos, Cover, pp. 14, 16–17, 17, 19, 20–21, 22–23, 23, 29, 35, 36 (top), 42, 43, 55, 59, 63

About the Author

Susan Sexton has always enjoyed reading books. She grew up reading mysteries, adventures, and biographies. As a child, her favorite book was *The Witch of Blackbird Pond*. Now Ms. Sexton is fulfilling a longtime dream—writing books.

Ms. Sexton taught elementary students for several years in Missouri. She enjoys reading, writing, and traveling. She also loves spending time with her husband and children and their pets—Tally, a golden retriever; Sammy, a cat; and Spikey, an iguana.

Printed in the United States of America. For information, contact Perfection Learning® Corporation, 1000 North Second Avenue, P.O. Box 500, Logan, Iowa 51546-0500.
Tel: 1-800-831-4190 • Fax: 1-800-543-2745
perfectionlearning.com
Paperback ISBN 0-7891-5877-9
Cover Craft® ISBN 0-7569-1039-0

2 3 4 5 6 7 PP 11 10 09 08 07 06

Table of Contents

Chapter 1

A Hardworkin' Man

Bob Glidden wants to be remembered in racing circles for what he is—a hard worker. He and his family work at racing seven days a week.

Bob was a line mechanic at a Ford dealership in the 1950s. He raced on weekends as a hobby. His wife and sons helped.

At first, Bob just raced for the trophies. But when he started winning races, he began winning money—just a little at first. But soon, his wins began to amount to something.

Bob and his wife had to make a decision. Should he leave racing or quit his job? If Bob quit his job, he'd have to make a living at racing.

The couple chose racing. It was a good choice. Bob held the record for the most National Hot Rod Association (NHRA) wins for many years!

All the family helped in one way or another. But Bob was the main guy. He drove the dragsters. And he also was the head mechanic.

After a day of racing, Bob would be seen under the car. He'd be adjusting or fixing the car himself—even after he became a **professional**!

Bob won the NHRA National Pro Stock race 84 times! In 10 of those, he was World Champion!

And they're off!

Drag Racing

Drag racing is just one of many auto-racing sports. People all across the United States drag race. There might even be people in your neighborhood or town who race!

You don't have to be a professional to drag race. In fact, most drag racers are **amateurs**. They may win a little money racing. But most just like to drive fast cars!

Becoming a drag racer can be as simple as having a **street car** and the money for entry fees. Or it can be as involved as needing thousands of dollars for a car, extra tires, extra engines, parts, a **pit** crew, and many other things.

Rookies often start out simple. Many of them use their own cars, trucks, or vans. These are the same ones they drive to work, to the store, and other places around town. These drivers take their street cars to the races. They drive against other street-car racers.

Drivers who have the racing "bug" often want bigger and better cars. They spend money on **hot rods** or **dragsters** that go much faster than street cars.

If you know people who have the racing bug, you know where to find them. They're at the drag strip on race days and at the garage in between!

People of all ages enjoy drag racing. Racers can be as young as eight years old. They can be the age of your grandparents. And they can be any age in between.

Dragster drivers have to think and act fast. The drivers are known as *drag racers, rodders, hands,* or *shoes.* The best drivers are called *hot shoes*!

Drag racing is racing in a straight line. It is a race between two cars.

The racetrack is $^1/_4$ mile long for adult drag racers and $^1/_8$ mile long for Jr. Dragsters (those 16 years old and younger). The winner is the racer who crosses the finish line first.

Once you've learned a little about drag racing, you may want to try it. You may want to feel the rush of racing down the track to win!

Chapter 2

Beating the Boys!

A woman in a dragster? No way!

That was the attitude of many drag racers and racing officials in the 1960s and early 1970s. But Shirley Muldowney had **grit**. But more than that, she had talent!

Shirley had to prove that she had what it took to be a drag racer. She did that and more!

Shirley was born in 1940 in New York. She began racing at a young age—just like most racers. She raced on the backstreets of her upstate New York hometown.

She learned what to do and what *not* to do in a race car. Her early learning, successes, talent, and love of racing are what made her a successful professional drag racer.

Shirley started her racing career in a gas dragster. But it wasn't long before she moved into **Funny Cars**. After that, she started racing **Top Fuelers**.

At first, other people in the sport—all men—weren't happy about a woman racing Top Fuelers. Not many women were in the sport of drag racing at the time. And the men had a hard time getting used to it.

Besides, Shirley was a mother. The men involved in drag racing wondered what would happen if she were hurt. They were afraid that the sport would get a bad name.

But Shirley didn't give in. So finally, she was able to race with the big boys! She raced against great drivers. Don Garlits, Connie Kalitta, Gary Beck, and Dick LaHaie were just some of them.

Then in 1984, Shirley had a terrible accident. It nearly cost her her life!

At a speed of 250 miles per hour (mph), Shirley's car went out of control. She had broken bones in all of her fingers. She had a broken **pelvis**. Her left leg and her right ankle were broken too.

Shirley suffered other injuries from the crash. But luckily, she lived. After 18 months of **rehabilitation**, she was ready to race again!

In 1989, Shirley had an **elapsed time** (ET) of 4.974 at the Keystone Nationals. She was then in an **elite** club known as the Four-Second Club. There weren't many other drivers in that group!

As a Top Fueler, Shirley won 18 National Championships. She's won 9 runner-up positions. Shirley was inducted into the Racing Hall of Fame in 1990.

Shirley was a Top Fuel winner. But that's not the reason why she'll be remembered. Shirley Muldowney will be remembered for breaking the gender barrier in drag racing.

Jr. Drag Racing

For kids, the Jr. Drag Racing League (JDRL) is the place! Racers must be between the ages of 8 and 17 to compete in the JDRL.

There are about 130 tracks in North America that have JDRL programs. The NHRA can tell you if one is near you.

The racers in the JDRL use a track that is $1/8$ mile long. That's half the distance of the adult drag racing tracks. The racers drive Jr. Dragsters.

The Jr. Dragsters look just like the dragsters that adults drive—only half as big. But don't let that fool you. They're powered by 5-**horsepower** (hp) motors that can go more than 50 mph.

Drag racing can cost a lot of money. The Jr. Dragsters cost around $3,000. But then racers have to pay for helmets, special clothing, safety gear, fuel, and other equipment. And they must join JDRL and pay any entry fees on race day.

Even though Jr. Drag Racing can cost a lot of money, thousands of kids still race. Boys and girls compete in events all race season long.

The 8- and 9-year-old drag racers finish a race in an ET of 12.90 seconds. That's around 45 mph.

The older Jr. Dragsters may finish with an ET of 7.90 seconds. That's going nearly twice as fast as the younger racers!

At the end of each JDRL season, finals are held. The winners of these final races can win thousands of dollars in college scholarships.

Some JDRL racers move on to race as adults. Some even become professional drag racers. But most adults race just for fun.

Amateur Bracket Racing

Most drag racers are people who have other jobs during the week. They are amateur racers. They come to racetracks on weekends.

These drivers compete in bracket racing. Drivers race against other drivers within the same bracket, or class. A driver's bracket is based on his or her ET.

The fastest cars in bracket racing are in the Super-Pro bracket. Drivers in this bracket also have the fastest ET.

Each racetrack sets its own guidelines for the brackets. But at many racetracks, the Super-Pro class is for cars with ETs of 10.99 seconds and faster.

The next bracket is the Pro class. At many tracks, these are the drivers whose ETs are between 11.00 seconds and 12.99 seconds.

Drag racers whose ETs are between 13.00 seconds and 14.99 seconds compete in the Sportsman bracket.

In the Super-Pro, Pro, and Sportsman brackets, the winners usually receive money as prizes.

The last bracket is the Trophy class. The winner usually picks up a trophy but no money. The drivers in this class are usually new to the sport of drag racing. At many tracks, these racers have ETs of more than 14.99 seconds.

Bracket racers don't always add special parts to their cars to make them run faster and better. Some bracket racers just race their everyday street cars.

Brackets
- Super-Pro
- Pro
- Sportsman
- Trophy Class

But other racers do add **high-performance** parts to their cars to make them go faster. And some racers drive cars that are built only for racing.

Bracket racing is designed so that unequal cars can race against one another. A regular street car can race against a specially built car. Or perhaps a driver will race against another driver whose car is faster.

In bracket racing, the slower cars and regular street cars still have a chance to win.

Bracket racing has special rules designed to make all cars equal. These rules were developed by the NHRA.

Some tracks may have policies about bracket racing that are different from other tracks. But the final authority on bracket racing is the NHRA bracket-racing rules.

Bracket races are set up so that the faster cars have a **handicapped** start. This means that the slower cars leave the starting line first.

Other sports use handicaps too. In golf and bowling, handicaps are used in scoring. The better the golfer or bowler, the lower his or her handicap.

Handicaps make sports more equal for people of differing abilities. Handicaps also challenge the better players to continue to play their best and not slack off.

This is how handicapped starts work in drag racing.

Racers run **time trials**. Only one driver races to the finish line. The time trials tell the driver what his or her ET is each time. After running a few time trials, the driver can then get a good idea of how fast his or her car can go.

The drivers then choose ETs they think they can run during a race. This elapsed time is a **dial-in**. The drivers write their dial-ins on their car windshields and side windows with white shoe polish. Once the drivers have chosen dial-ins, they can't run races any faster than the ETs they've chosen.

For example, if a driver chooses a dial-in of 12.07 seconds, he or she can't run the race any faster than that. The driver can run 12.07 seconds or slower—just not faster.

If a driver runs a race faster than his or her dial-in, it is a **breakout**. Drivers who break out automatically lose their races.

When two cars race, they may have different dial-ins. The one with the slower dial-in leaves the starting line first.

For example, one driver has a dial-in of 11.50 seconds. The other driver has a dial-in of 15.50 seconds. The driver with a dial-in of 15.50 seconds leaves the starting line first.

To determine how much of a head start the slower driver gets, the dial-ins must be compared. In the example above, there is a difference between the dial-ins of 4 seconds (15.50 seconds − 11.50 seconds = 4 seconds).

The slower car gets to leave the starting line 4 seconds earlier than the faster car. That's a handicapped start for the faster car. If both cars break out, the driver who went over his or her dial-in by the least amount is the winner.

Handicaps, dial-ins, and breakouts are what make bracket racing interesting. They keep races more equal for cars of differing abilities. And it keeps the drivers on their toes!

Pro Stock Pontiac during time trials

Drag Racing Classes

There are over 200 classes of race cars in NHRA competition. These classes are grouped into 11 car categories. Each category has its own NHRA rules. And the rules for each category are different.

The NHRA rules tell what type of car, what engine size, and what car weight belong in each group. Also, the NHRA tells drivers within the groups what changes they can and cannot make to the cars.

Not all drag racing is bracket racing! Professional drivers and some amateur drivers don't need handicaps. The drivers they're racing against don't need handicaps either.

These racers have a heads-up start. That's where both cars leave the starting line at the same time.

There are three professional groups of drag racing cars. They are Top Fuel, Funny Car, and Pro Stock.

There are five drag racing groups for amateurs that use a heads-up start. They are Federal-Mogul Dragster, Federal-Mogul Funny Car, Super Comp, Super Gas, and Super Street.

The remaining groups, Competition, Super Stock, and Stock, are made up of many subclasses. These groups have bracket racing.

Drag racing classes are grouped into 11 categories.

Pro	Amateur	Bracket
Top Fuel	Federal-Mogul Dragster	Competition
Funny Car	Federal-Mogul Funny Car	Super Stock
Pro Stock	Super Comp	Stock
	Super Gas	
	Super Street	

Professional/Heads-Up Drag Racing

Top Fuel Dragsters

The Top Fuel dragsters are long, skinny cars. They're the only drag racers that don't look like regular cars. Some people have made up nicknames for the Top Fuel dragsters—rails, diggers, and slingshots.

You won't see Top Fuelers cruising around town. These dragsters are built just for drag racing. With their 5,000 hp motors, the cars can cover the $1/4$-mile distance of the track in less than 5 seconds!

In 1988, Eddie Hill became the first Top Fuel racer to finish in less than 5 seconds. He had an ET of 4.990 seconds!

In 1992, Kenny Bernstein topped the record with an ET of 4.794 seconds!

The Top Fuel dragsters can reach speeds of more than 300 mph! In 1992, Kenny Bernstein also broke the 300 mph barrier. He reached a speed of 301.7 mph! Bernstein traveled more than 300 mph two more times that season.

Top Fuelers must weigh at least 2,150 pounds including the driver's weight. They are usually about 25 feet long. They're only 3 feet wide and 3 feet high. They have huge, thick back tires, or slicks. The front tires are very small.

Most of the car, including where the driver sits, can only be 2 inches off the ground. But from the front of the car to

12 inches behind the front axle, the car must be 3 inches off the ground.

A Top Fuel dragster has a wing that sticks up from the back. The wing is called an airfoil. And there's a **spoiler** on the front. The airfoil and spoiler help keep the car on the ground as it speeds toward the finish line.

The driver sits in the **roll cage**. The huge engine is right behind the driver. The steering wheel in a dragster is shaped like a butterfly.

Top Fuel dragsters use a special fuel called **nitromethane**, or nitro. Nitro costs more than $1,000 for a 50-gallon drum. A Top Fueler will use about $2^1/_2$ drums during a typical race weekend!

Top Fuelers have brakes only on the rear wheels. Since the cars travel at very high speeds, they are difficult to stop after races. These dragsters have parachutes that pop out to help the cars slow down and stop. Some dragsters even have two chutes!

Funny Cars

Funny Cars look like cars you might see on the street. But they're made just for drag racing! It is illegal to drive a Funny Car on the street.

When a racing announcer first saw the cars, he thought they looked funny. That's how they got their unusual name!

The doors, windows, hood, and trunk on a Funny Car don't even open. They're fake! So how does the driver climb inside?

The body of a Funny Car opens up like a giant clam. The body is made of **fiberglass**. It's very lightweight. The entire body lifts up from the front. A pole is used to prop it up and keep it from falling down.

The driver can climb inside from under the body. He or she sits in a seat where the backseat should be. In case of emergency, there's a small door in the roof. The driver can get out quickly if needed.

The body and roof area must have a special coating. This coating keeps fire from spreading if there's a crash or the motor blows up.

A Funny Car must weigh at least 2,325 pounds, including the driver's weight. The front of the car is 3 inches from the ground. The rest of it is only 2 inches off the ground! The front end of the car slopes toward the ground.

The frames and motors of Funny Cars are similar to those of Top Fuelers. But the frames are a little smaller. And the motors have less horsepower. They burn nitro like a Top Fueler. Or they can use alcohol or gas.

Wheelie bars

Funny Cars have **wheelie bars** behind them. These bars have small wheels mounted to stick out in back of the dragster. This helps to keep the front end from flying up in the air and the dragsters from flipping over backward.

Most Funny Cars are a little slower than the Top Fuel dragsters—but not by much! They travel more than 300 mph! In 1993, Chuck Etchells broke the 5.0-second barrier in his Funny Car. He had an ET of 4.986 seconds!

Then in 1994, John Force did even better! He broke the ET record by running a 4.939!

Because they go so fast, Funny Cars have brakes on both the front and back wheels. And they need parachutes to help them stop.

Pro Stock

Pro Stock cars look like regular cars. But they're changed to make them go faster. Some people call them muscle cars.

The body of a Pro Stock car is made of steel. But the hood, trunk, and front fenders are plastic. Including the driver, Pro Stock cars must weigh at least 2,350 pounds.

The Pro Stock cars can be no more than five years old. They must be a two- or a four-door car. The car and motor must have been made in North America.

Some drivers take out the instruments on the dash of the car. Some drivers leave them in. Others paint the dash so that it looks as though there are instruments.

A Pro Stock driver sits where the driver's seat is. All the cars have **roll bars** and roll cages. The windows are made of safety glass. These safety items help protect the drivers in crashes.

Pro Stock cars burn alcohol or gasoline. They don't go as fast as the Top Fuelers or the Funny Cars. But they can travel more than 190 mph. They can travel the $1/4$-mile strip in 7 seconds.

Many different models are Pro Stock cars. NHRA officials group the cars according to their model, weight, horsepower, and transmission. This way, cars that are similar will race each other in heads-up starts.

Amateur/Heads-Up Drag Racing

In the past, people paid more attention to professional racing. Amateur races were not followed as much.

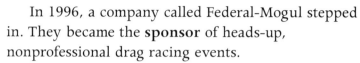

In 1996, a company called Federal-Mogul stepped in. They became the **sponsor** of heads-up, nonprofessional drag racing events.

Federal-Mogul sponsors Dragster and Funny Car events. It also sponsors other amateur heads-up and bracket-racing events. This sponsorship creates a wider audience for the amateur racers. It also increases the prize money for the winners.

> Federal-Mogul is a Michigan-based company. It manufactures and distributes precision auto and truck parts worldwide. Champion spark plugs and Anco wiper blades are among its products.

Federal-Mogul Dragsters

These dragsters look just like Top Fuel dragsters. But they don't burn nitro. They burn **methanol**.

Federal-Mogul dragsters travel more than 250 mph. They speed down the $\frac{1}{4}$-mile drag strip in less than 5.5 seconds!

Federal-Mogul Funny Cars

These Funny Cars look just like the nitro-burning Funny Cars. But like the dragsters, they burn methanol.

The Federal-Mogul Funny Cars must weigh at least 2,000 pounds. They can reach speeds of more than 250 mph. They travel the length of the drag strip in about 5.5 seconds.

Super Comp

The Super Comp class is for gas-burning dragsters. These dragsters are the fastest of the three Super classes. The drivers must not finish the race any quicker than 8.90 seconds.

Drivers can change their engines however they want.

Super Gas

Super Gas cars are like the ones you would see on the street. Few changes have been made to the body of these cars.

This class has the same rules as the Super Comp. But the drivers must not finish any quicker than 9.90 seconds.

Super Street

The Super Street class is for people new to the sport of drag racing. The Super Street cars aren't supposed to be changed. They're to be raced as they are— just as they were when they came from the factories.

Cars, vans, and trucks can participate in Super Street drag racing. But they can't finish any quicker than 10.90 seconds.

Amateur/Bracket Drag Racing

Competition

Competition drag racing has 42 different classes. The different classes are for the different styles of cars.

Some are dragsters—the long, skinny racers. Some are regular cars that have been changed to go faster. Some are regular two- and four-door cars.

The motors for the different Competition cars are different too. Some are the small four cylinders. Some are powerful V-6 and V-8 motors.

Competition cars within each class have differing abilities. The drivers also have different skills. So Competition racers use the handicapped start, or bracket racing.

All of the cars in Competition drag racing burn gasoline.

Super Stock drag lifts the front wheels.

Super Stock

There are also many different types of Super Stock cars. Some are made in the United States. Some are made in other countries.

Super Stock cars must look the way they did when they came from the auto factories. Drivers can't make many changes to these cars.

There are 83 different groups of cars and trucks in the Super Stock class. Some are cars like you would see on the road today. Some are the muscle cars from the 1960s and 1970s.

Super Stock cars also use a handicapped starting system. The drivers must write their dial-in on the car windows. In this way, all racers have a chance of winning.

Stock

Stock cars are cars that haven't been changed in any way. They're like the cars that you see every day on the street. They're like the car your family may own.

Racers drive cars that are made in the United States or other countries.

There are 80 different groups of cars in the Stock class. Some people race the cars they drive to work. Others race trucks or muscle cars.

As with the Competition and Super Stock classes, the Stock class also uses a handicapped start. This way, even new racers have a chance to win.

Other Types of Drag Racing

Motorcycle Racing

In the 1960s, the NHRA added motorcycle drag racing events. The bikes must weigh at least 600 pounds including the driver. Many types of motorcycles drag race. Harley-Davidsons are made in Milwaukee, Wisconsin. A special group was formed just for Harley racers. It is called the American Motorcycle Racing Association (AMRA). Harley riders also race in NHRA events.

But there are other types of racing bikes. Yamaha, Kawasaki, Suzuki, and Honda motorcycles participate in Pro Stock Bike drag races.

In the NHRA events, bikes must have been made in 1993 or later. They can't be changed too much. They have to look like the bikes you see on the street. And the engine and body style must be the same.

All motorcycles must pass an inspection before they race. Officials make sure the bikes are safe to ride. And they make sure the drivers follow the rules.

Other racing organizations hold drag racing events for Top Fuel bikes. This means that they use nitro. Top Fuel bikes travel as fast as 230 mph in less than 7 seconds!

Some racing bikes use wheelie bars. The bars stick out from the back of the bike. These bars help keep the front of the bikes from lifting into the air.

Some motorcycle dragsters need more than twice the length of the racing strip to stop. Some even need parachutes!

Truck Racing

The NHRA also sponsors Pro Stock Truck drag racing. The trucks must have been made in 1996 or later. They can be from the United States or other countries.

The pickup trucks used in Pro Stock Truck racing have extended cabs. The trucks must weigh at least 2,300 pounds, including the driver.

Other Racing

Other types of drag racing events are held all over the world. Organizations like the International Hot Rod Association (IHRA) sponsor car and truck drag racing. The International Drag Bike Association (IDBA) sponsors motorcycle drag racing events. And the National Drag Boat Association (NDBA) sponsors drag boat racing.

Chapter 3

Art Chrisman's Hustler

Art Chrisman was born in Arkansas in 1929. He discovered fast cars after his family moved to California.

When Art was in college in California, he'd race on the streets. But he and his friends were ticketed for speeding. Plus racing on the streets was dangerous.

As more people became interested in drag racing, they found safe, legal places to race. On just about any Sunday, Art would be at the Santa Ana track. He'd work on his car all week. And then he'd race the next Sunday!

Art's brother, Lloyd, **tuned up** the car with Art's help. Then Art would race to victory! He was a **dominant** force in drag racing in the early days.

In 1958, Art built a nitro dragster. He named it the Hustler after an old airplane.

In 1959, the Hustler traveled the $^1/_4$ mile at 181.81 mph. It was one of the first cars to ever go that fast. And it was one of the best dragsters ever!

Art liked making new racing creations as much as he enjoyed racing. One car had two motors and six wheels. One motor ran an outside set of wheels. The other ran an inside set of wheels. Another car had four motors.

Back then, the racers and teams made their own cars out of whatever they could find—and whatever they could make work.

But now, all cars are pretty much the same. One dragster looks just like another. And Funny Cars all look alike. The only differences are the colors, sponsors, and a few minor things.

One thing about Art's interesting cars, though, was that he built them to be safe.

Art retired from racing in 1962. He was raising a family. Back then, racing just wasn't a sport in which one could make a living.

So Art went to work for Ford Motor Company. He worked there for 10 years.

In 1997, Art was inducted into the Motorsports Hall of Fame.

Art Chrisman and the Hustler are still names people recognize. One is a champion driver. The other is the best car Chrisman ever made and one of the best dragsters ever to race!

"The Hustler"

The History of Drag Racing

Drag racing began in the 1930s in southern California. Car factories were building powerful cars. And the drivers liked to test the power of their cars.

The drivers tested their cars on the city streets. If two powerful cars pulled up to a stoplight or stop sign at the same time, they looked for a race. The drivers glanced at each other. And they probably **revved up** their engines.

Then when the light turned green or a signal was given, the cars raced forward. Side by side, the drivers raced to the next block or to the next light.

Sometimes, when the drivers took off, the front ends of their cars would pop up in the air in a **wheelie**. This caused the back ends to drag on the ground. Some people think this is how the term *drag racing* began.

Racing on the city streets was dangerous. The racers and other drivers were sometimes hurt in crashes.

Soon, laws were passed to ban this type of racing. With the help of parents and police, racing on city streets stopped. Adults helped find new places for the drag races.

Older model street drag

Away from the city, stretches of road were marked for racing. People sometimes raced on airport runways or on dry lake beds.

The Bonneville Salt Flats in Utah was a favorite racing place. People still race there today. Many land speed records have been set on the flats!

People began forming drag racing clubs. The people would get together to work on their cars. They would talk about the best kinds of tires or motor parts.

The clubs began racing against one another. The first organized drag racing event was in Santa Ana, California, in 1950. Thousands of people came to an airstrip to watch the races.

But the drag racers knew there was still a need for safety improvements. So in 1951, the NHRA was formed. The NHRA created the rules and standards for safe drag racing.

Other drag racing groups formed, such as the IHRA and the American Hot Rod Association (AHRA). But it was the NHRA that started organizing races and implementing safety features.

One of the first things that the NHRA did was to create classes of racing. They formed the classes based on body style and motor size.

Until then, the same few cars won all of the races. Drag racing was now fair for everyone.

The NHRA's first national event was held in 1955. About 300 people entered the race.

Now the NHRA holds 20 national events annually. Some events have more than 1,000 people who want to race!

The NHRA also oversees weekend or bracket racing. These are the races held at local tracks all over the United States.

Vintage open-wheeled street drag

Chapter 4

"Brute Force"

Brute Force

John Force is one of the most popular drivers in drag racing. He is not just popular for his skill at drag racing. He is also a **showman**.

John is a storyteller. He loves to tell stories about his own racing. And people love to listen.

John was born in May 1949 in Southern California. He drove trucks for a living. His first racing experience was in Australia at the age of 25.

John began racing NHRA Funny Cars in 1978. But it was four years later that he won his first National event as a Funny Car driver. He beat Ed McCulloch to take the win.

In the early 1990s, John suffered several crashes. But

incredibly, he climbed out of each mangled or burned car unhurt!

But the crashes seemed to affect John. He had a fire wall built around where he sat in the cockpit. He had several fire extinguishers mounted in his car. And he even talked about building a Funny Car with a rear engine.

But even with these safety measures, John still had crashes. He pushed himself and his car too hard. He wanted to break records every time he climbed into his car!

33

So in 1993, John took a look at earlier seasons. He began to rethink the way he was driving. John decided to focus on winning a championship, not just breaking records.

In 1993, John won 11 races. This was a new personal record! And he won 5 of the races in a row!

John also made the finals 13 times in just 18 races. And he won the championship by more than 4,000 points!

John was finally looking at the big picture. He wasn't focused on individual races or breaking records. His goal was to win the championship. And he succeeded!

John is now the professional driver with the most NHRA wins. He has won 92 times. He also has won more Funny Car drag races than any other professional driver.

He was the first Funny Car driver to **exceed** 320 mph. He ran 323.35 mph in 1998! He won the Ollie award that year too. The award was given to John by *Car Craft* magazine for his lifetime achievement in racing.

John has brought a lot to the sport of drag racing. And here's hoping he will continue racing for many years to come!

Ins and Outs of the Dragster

The frame of a dragster is the **chassis**. All the parts are attached to the frame.

The body is the outside of the car. It covers the frame and other parts. The body protects the driver and spectators from the moving parts. And it protects the driver from flying rocks and during crashes.

Drivers like to decorate the bodies of their dragsters. A driver might paint the dragster bright colors and add his or her name and the team's name.

Many professional and sportsmen drivers have sponsors. These drivers always put their sponsors' names on the cars.

The sponsors help pay for upkeep of the cars and the

drag racing events. In return, the sponsors get to advertise their businesses on the cars!

And some drivers like to give their cars names. They paint their cars' names on the bodies too.

John Force's car is Brute Force. Art Chrisman's dragster was named the Hustler. And racing great Connie Kalitta called his car the Bounty Hunter.

Dragsters use special tires, or slicks. These tires don't have tread on them like tires on family cars. Their slick surfaces help the dragsters get good **traction** on the track. This means that the tires grip the surface. And dragsters need good traction to go fast!

The front tires don't need traction. In fact, they are sometimes up in the air! Some dragsters use motorcycle tires.

Super Gas Chevelle drag car pops the front wheels.

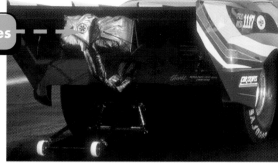

And some use regular car tires up front.

Sometimes, the fronts of dragsters pop into the air as the cars jump forward on the green light. If the drivers aren't careful, the cars could flip over. So many drivers use wheelie bars.

Because dragsters travel so fast, brakes alone aren't going to stop them. So, many dragsters have parachutes to help them stop.

The parachute is folded up and mounted behind the driver's head. After the drivers cross the finish line, they pull a cord. The parachutes are released. Some drivers even have two parachutes!

The stopping force of a parachute is very strong! If a driver pops the chute when traveling 280 mph, he feels a negative force of 7Gs (gravity). That means the driver feels a force that is seven times the force of gravity! Imagine the force of two chutes!

Once the chute slows down the dragster, the driver steps on the brakes. The driver's team is waiting at the end of the shut-down area. The crew gathers up the chute. That way, it won't be damaged by dragging on the ground.

The dragster's engine is very powerful. It needs a lot of power to accelerate fast.

Regular cars have about 150 hp. But some dragsters have over 4000 hp!

Dragsters have the same type of motors that regular cars have. But they are made to create more power. And the motors run on nitro, alcohol, or regular gas.

Drag racing cars have many other parts. Some are the same as on regular cars. But some parts have been added to give the car more power.

Modified cars have been changed a little to drag race. Altered cars have been changed a lot. Modifying or altering a car improves its abilities.

You won't find these cars on the street! You'll have to go to the track to see them.

Professional racers usually have crews who keep their cars in top shape. The crew is a very important part of the racing team. The racers can't make it without their crews! "Wrenches" are the people in the crew. The crew leader is the "chief wrench."

Most amateur drivers work on their own cars. Or they may have a few friends to help them.

Chapter 5

"Big Daddy"

It was the year 1970. The drag strip in Long Beach, California, was a busy place. "Big Daddy" Don Garlits was ready to roll!

As Don pushed on the gas pedal, his Top Fuel dragster shot down the strip. He was gaining speed as he neared the finish line.

But then something shocking happened! Don's transmission blew up. His dragster was torn in half!

The half Don was in rolled on down the track. It finally came to a stop with Don lying on his back in the seat. He was looking up at his feet. Or what was left of them!

Some of Don's toes and part of one foot were cut off. When the transmission blew up, parts of it had flown through the air. That's how Don's foot was injured.

Up until then, Don and all the other dragster racers had cars with the motors sitting in front of the driver. That was dangerous. So Don changed all that.

Rather than leave drag racing, Don stayed. He wanted to work to make the sport safer for the drivers.

So Don designed a car with the motor in back of the driver. Then, if the motor blew up, it wouldn't hurt the driver.

At first, people didn't believe that the new car would win any races. But in 1971, Don won his first NHRA event ever. The same year, he took the AHRA title!

Within one year, all of the major Top Fuel racers went to a rear engine.

Don Garlits has made a big impact on the sport. He is known for working to make the sport safer. He's also worked hard to make the Top Fuelers go faster.

Don was born in January of 1932. He didn't grow up wanting to be a racer. He grew up on a farm. He milked cows seven days a week. So he didn't really have time for cars.

But soon, he left the farm to make more money. He went to work at an auto body shop. He didn't know anything about cars. But he learned quickly.

Don started racing a little bit in Florida. With a little pushing from others, he began to race more. And he started winning.

Don was the first driver to reach 200 mph from a standing start in the $1/4$ mile. He was also the first driver to ever go 250 mph and 270 mph!

In 1987, Don's car, the Swamp Rat XXX, went on display in the Smithsonian Institute. It is now part of the National Museum of American History in Washington, D.C.

"Swamp Rat"

In 1992, Don announced his retirement. He had suffered an eye injury during a practice run. He didn't want to lose his sight, so he quit racing.

During his racing career, Don won the AHRA Championship 10 times. He won the IHRA Championship once. And he won the NHRA Championship 3 times. Big Daddy has the best all-around record in drag racing!

Getting Ready to Race!

In order to compete in adult drag racing events, drivers must be at least 16 years old with valid driver's licenses. And they must have cars in good racing shape.

Racers find a drag strip near them. They may have to look online or in a phone book. They can browse through drag racing books and magazines. Or they can just ask around.

When a racer has found a track, he or she should get some information about the dates and times of racing events.

Once a driver arrives at the track, an entry fee is paid. This fee admits the driver and the car into the track. If the racer brings along a crew, each member will have to pay for a pit pass.

When drivers pay to enter a race, they are given blank tech-inspection cards for recording information about their cars. This information includes a brief description of the car and details the motor.

Then each car will have a tech inspection. An inspector makes sure the car is safe to race. The inspector also looks for car parts that might fly off during a race!

The inspector will probably check to make sure the windows roll up. The windows can protect drivers in crashes. He'll check the seatbelt. This is required equipment for the drivers.

Drivers are asked to sign release forms. Signing the form means that drivers won't hold the racetrack responsible if they get hurt.

Release forms may sound scary. But they remind drivers that racing is serious business. And drivers should do what they can to be safe.

Using white shoe polish, the inspector will write a number on each car. This number will appear on the windshield and side window.

The car number is important to a lot of people. The announcer can spot the car when announcing the race or relaying information. Race officials can give drivers printouts of times and speeds at the end of their runs.

Once cars have been inspected, drivers head to the pits. This is where drivers stay until it's time to line up for time trials and racing. It's also where they work on their cars if they need to.

During time trials, drivers take practice trips down the drag strip. They work on watching the **Christmas tree**. And they get a good idea of how fast their cars are running. Knowing this helps bracket racers figure out a good dial-in.

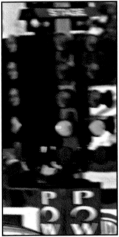

The pits are a good place to talk to other racers. New drivers can find out what works best for other drivers. They can also see what other drivers do to their cars to make them run better. And it's also just a good place to talk about the sport of drag racing.

Once drivers are in the pits, they have to pay attention. They must listen for the announcer to call their class to the staging lanes. These are numbered lanes where cars line up.

The track officials tell drivers which lane to go to. Here drivers will wait until it's their turn to race.

Bracket drivers need to have their dial-ins written on their windshields. This helps the track officials as they line up the cars in the staging lanes.

As each driver begins his turn, he will head toward the burnout pit. Cars with wide, slick tires spin their tires in water. This helps clean any dirt, rocks, or oil from them. And it heats up the tires for racing. Hot tires grip the track better.

In the 1960s, drivers drove through bleach in the burnout pit. But this often caused fires. So tracks began using water.

Street-car drivers don't usually spin their tires. Because of the design of street tires, a burnout won't help. But there are ways to heat and clean street tires.

While pressing on the brake or **clutch**, drivers rev up their motors. They floor the gas pedal while releasing the brake or clutch. The tires heat as they spin on the asphalt or concrete. Since this is done outside the burnout area, drivers must be careful not to hit the cars around them!

If drivers warm their tires once, they should warm them again before each pass down the track. If they don't, it could affect their driving.

Once a driver is at the Christmas tree, it's time to race!

Drag warming the tires

Safety

Don Garlits and many other drivers and mechanics have worked to make drag racing a safe sport. It's safer than most other kinds of car racing. But there are some dangers.

Drag racing cars must have safety features. If they don't have them, they can't race.

Dragsters have big engines. They can catch fire or blow up. Then the engine parts fly through the air. The driver can get hurt—like Don Garlits. People watching the races can get hurt too.

Cars are required to have thick metal shields between the drivers and the engines. If the engines blow or catch fire, the drivers are protected.

Some dragsters even have fire walls built in their cars. A fire wall is a shield made of special material that won't catch on fire. It protects the driver from heat and flames.

Some dragsters also have fire extinguishers. Some go off automatically if there's a crash. On some dragsters, the drivers must pull a cord on the extinguishers. That releases the contents to put out any fires.

Another safety feature is the roll cage. A roll cage is made of steel. It is mounted to the chassis. And the driver sits inside.

A roll bar is also mounted to the frame of the car. It is a curved piece of metal. And it goes from one side of the car to the other, right over the driver's head.

Sometimes, dragsters roll over or flip upside down. If that happens, roll cages and roll bars protect drivers from getting hurt.

Dragsters also have soft foam or padding inside the cars. This adds protection for drivers if they are knocked around inside the car.

Drag racing cars also need much stronger seat belts than the ones in family cars. They will probably be five-point belts with crotch straps.

That means that the belt goes over the shoulders. And it attaches near the hips and between the legs. The straps then come together near the driver's chest.

The straps are about 3 inches wide. And they must be pulled very tight. Some drivers need help strapping themselves in order to get the belts tight enough!

Even if a driver is in his street car for bracket racing, he is required to wear a seatbelt. A track official will remind the driver if he or she forgets.

Some dragsters have open cockpits. That means areas around the drivers aren't fully enclosed. So these drivers need arm straps. They keep the drivers' arms in the cars in the event of a crash.

The drivers wear special safety gear. NHRA requires that drivers that race 13.99 seconds or faster must wear helmets. A full face helmet works well. It protects the head and face from flying objects and fire.

Some drivers wear a regular helmet. Then they wear safety goggles to protect their eyes.

Drivers in the slower classes sometimes wear helmets. And they wear sunglasses or safety glasses to protect their eyes. And that's a good idea!

In most classes, drivers must wear special clothing. Their jackets, pants, and gloves must be fireproof. Or they may wear a one-piece fireproof suit. And some must wear fireproof shoes or boots.

Another required piece of safety equipment is a neck collar. It keeps the driver's head from flopping around and prevents neck injuries.

Top Fuelers and Funny Car drivers sometimes have to take tests. These tests show that the drivers can find the controls in their dragsters even if they're blindfolded!

Safety features weren't as critical in the early years of racing. But as the cars get bigger, faster, and more powerful, safety is a very important issue.

Chapter 6

The Snake

Don Prudhomme was given the nickname "Snake." He was tall and thin. And he was fast off the starting line. So Don won a lot of races.

Don didn't like the nickname very much. But it stuck with him. This nickname was painted along with his name on his dragsters.

Don had been racing for fun since his teens. And in 1962, Don won the Bakersfield championship at the young age of 20. It was his first year as a professional driver.

Don has driven Funny Cars and Top Fuelers. He retired in 1994 in the "Snake's Final Strike Tour."

At the time of his retirement, Don had won four NHRA Winston Cup Championships in a row, from 1975 to 1978. He also had the most NHRA wins at 49. Fourteen of those wins were in Top Fuel dragsters. And 35 of them were in Funny Cars.

Because Don was so quick off the line, he was able to record the first 5-second ET. In 1975, his Funny Car clocked in at 5.98!

In 1982, Don set another record. He traveled the quarter-mile in 5.63 seconds. And in 1989, he ran in less than 5.20 seconds!

Aside from the ET records, Don has also set speed records. In 1982, he was the very first driver to pass 250 mph. And at the age of 51, Don was just the third driver to pass 300 mph!

47

In 2001, the NHRA celebrated its 50th anniversary. At that time, Don was considered to be the third-greatest driver in drag racing history.

Even after he retired, the NHRA wanted Don to continue to be part of the sport. So Don now owns two racing teams.

Don owns a Top Fueler driven by Larry Dixon. He also owns a Funny Car driven by Ron Caps.

No matter what the year, Don will always be thought of as one of the best drag racers! Being fast off the line is the key to winning. And Don certainly mastered the skill as the Snake!

Ready, Set, Go!

So how do drivers know when to start down the track? Drag races used to start when a flagman waved a flag. Now electronic equipment and lights are used to start races. A series of lights, or Christmas tree, tells a racer when to start.

The Christmas tree is a series of yellow and green lights. The yellow lights appear first. These show that the drivers are ready. When the last green lights flash, the drag race is on!

As the drivers pull forward, they watch the Christmas tree. It sits 20 feet past the starting line.

At the top of the tree are two small yellow light bulbs. These are the pre-stage lights. And they're activated by beams running across each lane of the drag strip.

The pre-stage lights appear when the car's front tires are seven inches away from the starting line. And as the cars keep moving slowly forward, another set of yellow lights comes on.

These lights are the staging lights. These appear when the cars are at the starting line.

Now both cars are in position on the drag strip. The drivers have their cars pointed straight ahead. They're concentrating on the Christmas tree.

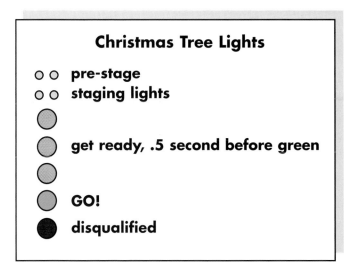

Christmas Tree Lights

○ ○ **pre-stage**
○ ○ **staging lights**

get ready, .5 second before green

GO!
disqualified

Drag strip lanes are divided with painted lines. Some have a guardrail or fence between them. This helps the drivers see where they need to be. And it helps keep cars from crashing into each other as they race down the strip!

As soon as both cars have their staging lights set, they wait. The starter pushes a button that controls the rest of the lights on the tree. And when the button is pushed, the countdown begins!

For professional drivers, the lights come on quickly. The next three lights are amber. And they come on at the same time. Then, less than .5 second later, the green lights come on.

It's the same for some of the better amateur drivers. They are the drivers who have a lot of experience and go from a heads-up start.

But for weekend bracket racing, the starting lights are different. With the handicapped starts, the Christmas tree lights light up one at a time. And they light up with just .5 second between them.

As soon as the green light lights up, the driver should be on his way!

Driver gets the green light.

The driver's reaction time to the green light is very important in drag racing. Reaction time is how long it takes for the driver to see that the light is green and then stomp on the gas.

Reaction time is measured and reported to each driver. This helps him or her know when to step on the gas pedal. And then the driver can come off the starting line even quicker the next time.

The perfect reaction time is .5 second. Drivers want to be as close to this time as possible! This is known as attacking the green!

However, if a car rolls forward too soon, a red light on the tree will light up. That means that the driver is disqualified. The race is over for him or her!

Getting a good reaction time without red-lighting takes a lot of practice. That's why so many drivers take practice runs. It helps them know when to launch from the starting line. And it helps them see how their cars handle.

Just like the pre-stage and stage beams, there are other beams on the track. These beams measure the driver's reaction time, ET, and speed.

The drivers pass these beams at 60 feet, 330 feet, 660 feet, 1000 feet, and the finish line. These beams will record a driver's ET at each of the points on the track.

Two speed traps are also set up on the track. One is at 66 feet after the starting line. And the other speed-timing device is set at the finish line. This lets drivers know how fast they were going at the beginning and end of each race.

As the last green light flashes, the two cars race side by side down the strip. The cars zoom 1,320 feet through the finish line.

Junior dragsters at the start line

Funny Car ready to drag

Then what? The cars will be going too fast to just stop at the finish line.

For the drivers' safety, there's a shut-down strip, or overrun, at the end of the drag strip. The shut-down strip is often twice as long as the drag strip!

Here cars can safely slow and brake to a stop. And it's where the Top Fuelers and Funny Cars will pop their chutes!

After the cars have slowed enough, the drivers pull over into a third lane. This is the return lane. It leads back to the pits.

Professional drivers and some of the faster-running cars use tow trucks. The trucks tow the race cars back to the pits.

But before the drivers return to the pits, they stop at the ET slip booth. The official in the booth gives each driver a readout of his racing information.

The slip tells the drivers' reaction times, ETs, and speeds measured at each point on the track. And most importantly, it tells who won the race!

The drivers are given two scores. The ET score tells how much time it took to go from start to finish. And the second score measures the top speed of the car.

The winner is the driver with the lowest ET score. And some drivers win by just fractions of a second!

In fact, some drivers win because they had a better reaction time. So you can see that every second, *and* fraction of a second, counts!

Once the winner is determined, he or she stays around to race again. The losers are done racing for the day.

Racing Champions

Connie Kalitta

Connie Kalitta drove Funny Cars for years. But he is probably best remembered for his Top Fuelers.

Connie never won an NHRA Top Fuel Championship. But he did finish third in the championship for 15 seasons.

In 1962, Connie broke the 180-mph speed record by traveling 180.36 mph!

Connie loved driving and winning in drag racing!

Joe Amato

Amato had to be one of the most superstitious drivers! He raced a Top Fuel dragster. And it was always stuffed full of good luck charms!

Joe had a four-leaf clover sewn into his driving suit. He wore Snoopy underwear. And he always did the exact same things the same way before each race. Doing things out of order would have been bad luck!

Joe's fans sent him things. And he would find places for them in his car. He considered them all to be good luck.

But it's not just luck that made Joe a winner. He had pure skill and talent!

Joe won more NHRA Top Fuel dragster events than any other driver! He was the first Top Fuel driver to go over 260 mph and 280 mph!

Joe's best ET was 4.516 seconds. And his best speed ever was 326.67 mph!

But in 2000, Joe announced his retirement from drag racing. He was having eye trouble. When the parachutes popped after a race, it would damage his eyes a little at a time. That's the same reason Don Garlits had to retire.

Joe decided that driving with eye problems was unsafe for him. It was unsafe for the other drivers too.

However, Joe continues to be involved in drag racing. He owns his own team now. He hired Darrell Russell to drive the dragster.

Other Drivers

There are many other drag racers to learn about. Among them are Kenny Bernstein, Eddie Hill, Gary Ormsby, Chris Karamesines. There are the Pedregon brothers (Tony, Frank, and Cruz), Rhonda Hartman-Smith, Cory McClenathan, and many others! One of them may beat Joe Amato's winning record. Or one may be the next John Force!

So get out to the track! See firsthand what drag racing is all about. And watch for the next big winner!

Vintage dragster

Chris Karamesines

Joe Amato & Darrell Russell

Cory McClenathan

Rhonda Hartman-Smith

Larry Nance

Afterword

Want to Know More?

If you're interested in becoming a drag racer, you should first learn about the sport.

Besides this book, your local library or bookstore has books about racing. And reading about drag racing is a good place to start. You can learn about special words used in drag racing

Larry Morgan **Warren Johnson** **Cruz Pedregon**

Ron Krisher **Kenny Bernstein** **Eddie Hill**

such as *staging*, *Christmas tree*, and *burnout*. You can learn about what it takes to get ready for a race!

The National Hot Rod Association (NHRA) is an organization that has helped make drag racing popular and safe. This group holds national races for professional drivers. The NHRA also oversees local weekend races for amateurs in towns across America.

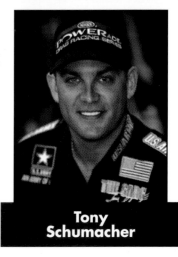

Tony Schumacher

You can contact the NHRA at the following address.
National Hot Rod Association
2035 Financial Way
Glendora, CA 91741
(626) 914-4761

Or to find out more information about the NHRA, visit its Web site: www.nhra.com. This Web site has current information about events, drivers, and teams. You can also learn about the Jr. Drag Racing League (JDRL).

Another group that supports drag racing events is the International Hot Rod Association (IHRA). This group hasn't been around as long as the NHRA. But they hold many of their own national events. They provide rules and support for some local racetracks.

You can reach the IHRA at the following address.
International Hot Rod Association
$9^1/_2$ E. Main Street
Norwalk, OH 44857
(419) 663-6666

More about the IHRA and IHRA-sponsored events can be found on the IRHA Web site: www.ihra.com.

There are also many other Web sites where you can find out more about the sport of drag racing. You can also learn about the teams and drivers.

Many professional drivers and teams have their own Web sites. You can read about the lives of famous drivers. You can also find their racing records, fastest times, and other information.

Another place to find information is at a track. You can find a list of tracks on the Internet or in your local telephone book. Look on the Internet or call the track to find out when races are held. You can almost always watch a race on the weekend.

You can learn a lot just by watching races. Watch what cars do before, during, and after the race. Also, many local racetracks let people walk through the pit areas.

In the pit area, you can see what drivers and teams do to the cars. If they're not busy, most drivers will talk with you about racing. And they'll answer your questions.

Drivers are glad to tell you what they know about the sport. And they love to show off their cars!

Some drag-racing tracks offer schools for drag racers. Classes are offered to help people who already race. Other classes are held for those new to the sport.

Drag-racing schools are great places to learn even more about the sport. They're also great places to find out if drag racing is right for you!

Glossary

amateur

person engaged in an activity or sport as a pastime, not as an occupation

breakout

in drag racing, act of racing faster than his or her predicted time

chassis

supporting frame of an automobile

Christmas tree

in drag racing, electronic starting device between the lanes on the starting line. It displays a light countdown for each driver.

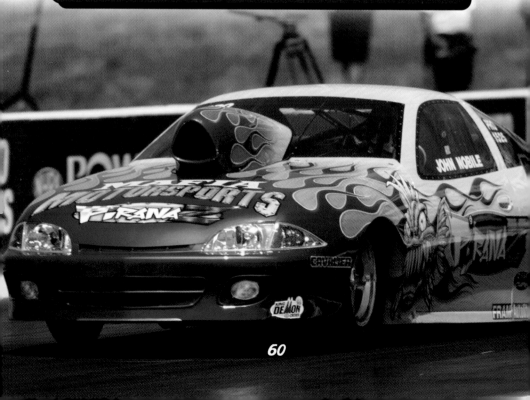

Pro Stock drag approaches the line during qualifying.

clutch

foot pedal next to the brake that engages and disengages a vehicle's transmission

dial-in

in drag racing, prediction of how quickly a vehicle will travel

dominant

most important

dragster

vehicle built or modified for use in a drag race

elapsed time (ET)

in drag racing, number of seconds and fractions of seconds it takes a car to move from a standing start to the finish line 1,320 feet ($^1/_4$ mile) away. The lower the ET, the faster the car!

elite

exclusive or selective

exceed

to go beyond

fiberglass

lightweight solid material often used to make auto bodies

Funny Car

specialized dragster (see separate entry) that has a one-piece molded body resembling the body of a mass-produced car

grit

courage in the face of hardship or danger

handicap

relating to a race or contest in which an advantage is given to one contestant to equalize chances of winning

high-performance

having superior quality and efficiency than that which is standard

horsepower

unit of power

hot rod

automobile that has been rebuilt or modified for high speed and fast acceleration

Glossary

methanol

light flammable, poisonous liquid alcohol used as a fuel

nitromethane (nitro)

liquid used as a fuel for rockets and high-performance (see separate entry) engines

pelvis

basin-shaped skeletal structure that rests on the lower limbs and supports the spinal column

pit

relating to the space alongside an auto racecourse used for refueling and repairing the cars during a race

professional

person engaged in an activity for pay

rehabilitation

act of restoring health

rev up

to increase the speed of an engine

roll bar

overhead metal bar on an automobile that is designed to protect the occupant in case of a rollover

roll cage

protective framework of metal bars enclosing the driver of a vehicle

rookie

first-year participant in a sport

showman

person with a sense or knack for giving a dramatic or entertaining presentation

spoiler

air deflector on an automobile to reduce the tendency to lift off the ground at high speeds

sponsor

person or organization that pays for or plans a project

street car

vehicle that is driven by a member of the general population; family vehicle

time trial

competitive event in which individuals are successively timed over a set course or distance. This occurs before the main event.

Top Fueler

fastest type of dragsters (see glossary entry), which is specially designed for the sport

traction

ability to grip something

tune up

general adjustment to make sure an engine is operating at top efficiency

wheelie

maneuver in which a wheeled vehicle is balanced on its rear wheel or wheels

wheelie bar

attachment to the back of vehicle that prevents excessive front-wheel lift

Super Stock Vette points its nose toward the sky.

Index